SUSAN B. ANTHONY

DARING TO VOTE

A Gateway Biography

BARBARA KEEVIL PARKER

The Millbrook Press
Brookfield, Connecticut

TO THE YOUNGER GENERATION
STACY, PAM, DONNA, MAKAYLA, AND ALEXANDRA
"CARRY ON"

10/04   gift

Thanks to Duane and Pam Parker, Dorothy Cotterell, Maureen Mitchell, Ilene Davey, Peggy Donnelly, Caitlin Farrell-Starbuck, Linda Brennan, and the children's librarians and resource staff at Barrington Public Library in Rhode Island for their help with this manuscript. And a special thanks to Laura Walsh, my editor.

Cover photograph courtesy of The Granger Collection, New York.
Photographs courtesy of: The Granger Collection, New York: pp. 7, 14, 26, 31, 41; Susan B. Anthony House, Rochester, N.Y.: p. 10; University of Rochester Library: pp. 13, 21; Culver Pictures: pp. 17, 24, 29; Picture Collection, The Branch Libraries, The New York Public Library: p. 33; North Wind Picture Archives: p. 34; AP/Wide World Photos: p. 42

Parker, Barbara Keevil.
Susan B. Anthony : daring to vote / Barbara Keevil Parker.
p.   cm. — (A Gateway biography)
Includes bibliographical references and index.
Summary: Presents the highlights of the life of a nineteenth-century crusader who spent much of her life involved in the temperance, abolitionist, and women's rights movements.
ISBN 0-7613-0358-8 (lib. bdg.)
1. Anthony, Susan B. (Susan Brownell), 1820–1906—Juvenile literature. 2. Feminists—United States—Biography—Juvenile literature. 3. Suffragists—United States—Biography—Juvenile literature. 4. Women—Suffrage—United States—History—Juvenile literature.
[1. Anthony, Susan B. (Susan Brownell), 1820-1906. 2. Feminists. 3. Women—Biography.
4. Women's rights.] I. Title. II. Series.
HQ1413.A55P37 1998 305.42'092—dc21 [B] 97-26310 CIP AC

Published by The Millbrook Press, Inc.
2 Old New Milford Road
Brookfield, Connecticut 06804

SUSAN B. ANTHONY

Would you vote if you thought you might go to jail?

Susan B. Anthony had two choices. She could stay home, obey the law, and leave voting to the men. Or she could register to vote, and break the law.

OCTOBER 1872

"Guelma! Look at this notice in today's newspaper!"

Susan's hand shook with excitement as she pointed to a notice for her older sister to read.

> Now register! Today and tomorrow are the only remaining opportunities....And yet, on election day, less than a week hence, hundreds of you are likely to lose your votes because you have not thought it worth while to give the five minutes....Register now!

Guelma frowned. "But you know that only men are allowed to register for voting."

"Until now!" Susan's lips pressed together in a defiant smile. Her jaw was fixed with iron determination. Susan grabbed her bonnet. "I'll be back later," she called to Guelma as she dashed out the door. She was on her way to pay a visit to some special women of Rochester, New York.

NOVEMBER 1, 1872

Early in the morning, fifty women quietly left their homes and headed to the voter registration offices around the city of Rochester. Susan, her sisters Guelma, Mary, and Hannah, plus twelve other women, entered a barber shop on West Street, the registration office of the Eighth Ward.

"We are here to register to vote," Susan told the startled election inspectors.

"That's impossible! Women are not allowed to vote!" the inspectors told them.

Susan refused to be turned away. "Allow me to read to you from the Fourteenth and Fifteenth Amendments to the U.S. Constitution.

> All persons born or naturalized in the United States…
> are citizens…
> The right of citizens of the United States to vote shall
> not be denied or abridged…on account of race,
> color, or previous condition of servitude [slavery].

"Do you see anything here that prohibits women from voting?" she asked.

The names of the women were entered on the voting list. Of the fifty women who attempted to register, only these sixteen, plus eight at other sites, were successful.

Even though it was known that women were not allowed to vote, many attempted to, citing the vague wording of the Fourteenth and Fifteenth Amendments to the Constitution. Here, a woman attempts to vote in New York City in 1871, but is unsuccessful. Susan B. Anthony was successful a year later, but was arrested soon after.

NOVEMBER 5, 1872 — ELECTION DAY

Sixteen women went to the polls in Rochester and voted for the president of the United States. At the age of fifty-two, Susan B. Anthony had waited long enough for the government to say that women could vote.

After voting, Susan returned to her home and wrote to her good friend Elizabeth Cady Stanton:

> Well, I have been and gone and done it! Positively voted…this morning at 7 o'clock; and swore my vote in at that.…Not a jeer, not a rude word, not a disrespectful look has met one woman. Now if all our suffrage women would work to this end…what strides we might make from now on!

NOVEMBER 28, 1872 — THANKSGIVING DAY

There was a knock on the door. Susan opened the door and found Chief Marshal E. J. Keeney.

"Good morning, Miss Anthony. Lovely day, isn't it?"

"What news do you bring, Mr. Keeney?"

"I apologize for this inconvenience, but I am here to deliver a warrant for your arrest. I also have warrants for your sisters."

Susan hid her surprise and coolly replied, "And for what crime are we being arrested?"

"You voted in an election, violating a federal law stating that anyone who votes without having the legal right to do so is guilty of a crime. You and your sisters will have to come to the office of the U.S. Commissioner of Elections here in Rochester. The ladies may walk by themselves," he mumbled. "I'll walk behind and no one will know what is happening."

"Absolutely not," Susan replied. "You will take me by force, Marshal, or not at all."

Mr. Keeney blushed. "I will not put handcuffs on you, but if you insist, I will accompany you to the election office."

"I insist!" she replied.

Marshal Keeney escorted her to the trolley. When asked for her fare Susan said defiantly, "I'm traveling at the expense of the government. This gentleman is escorting me to jail. Ask him for my fare."

A reluctant Marshal paid the fare.

All of the sixteen women who had voted on November 5 were arrested.

Why Did They Vote? In Susan B. Anthony's day, women had no rights. Every penny a woman earned had to be given to her husband. If she inherited property from her family, it became her husband's property. Children belonged to their fathers. Fathers could give their children away if they chose. Women who were beaten by their husbands had nowhere to go and no right to complain. But women did have to pay taxes on property they owned and could be brought to trial before an all-male jury and imprisoned or hanged if found guilty. They had no voice. Susan, representing many women, believed that unless women could vote, their pleas for equal treatment in other areas would be ignored.

Only Susan stood trial for voting illegally. As the leader, she represented all sixteen women. Her defense was based on the wording of the Fourteenth and Fifteenth Amendments to the Constitution. The amendments state that all people born in the United States are citizens, and that the right to vote cannot be denied to citizens. The Constitution did not specifically say that women could not vote.

From the time her trial date was set, Susan began a speaking tour. In January 1873 she attended the annual suffrage conven-

Between the time she was arrested in November 1872, and the start of her trial in June 1873, Susan traveled extensively to speak on behalf of woman suffrage. She was a popular speaker, and although she was declared guilty, she never paid her $100 fine.

tion in Washington, D.C. In February she spoke in Indiana. In May she went to New York City for the twenty-fifth anniversary of the first women's rights meeting at Seneca Falls, New York. At this convention the delegates passed a resolution declaring, "Not Susan B. Anthony but the government of the United States is on trial today."

Susan also toured all twenty-nine villages of her home county of Monroe, New York. Crowds came to hear her talk. Her speech was titled, "Is It a Crime for a Citizen of the United States to Vote?"

Because Susan's speeches were so popular, the district attorney was worried about her influence in Monroe County. The trial was moved to Canandaigua, in Ontario County, where Susan was thought to have less influence. Susan saw this as a challenge. She continued her speeches with the help of Matilda Joslyn Gage. Between them they covered thirty-seven districts in Ontario County in less than a month.

The trial began on June 17, 1873. Susan B. Anthony was not allowed to speak for herself. Her male attorney, the former judge Henry R. Selden, defended her. Judge Selden gave a magnificent three-hour argument for woman suffrage.

Nevertheless, the judge in the case bypassed the jury and declared her guilty of breaking the law.

> Any person…who shall vote without having a legal right to vote; or do any unlawful act to secure…an opportunity to vote for himself or any other person, shall be deemed guilty of a crime.

Susan was fined $100.

"I shall never pay a dollar of your unjust penalty," she declared. And she didn't.

Judge Hunt did not imprison her. He feared that she would appeal her case to the U.S. Supreme Court. He didn't want to take the chance that she might win.

Who was Susan B. Anthony, and why did she take so many risks just to vote?

Early Years. Adams, Massachusetts, was a tiny community tucked in the northern Berkshire Mountains. Here, Daniel Anthony, a Quaker, and Lucy Read, a Baptist, did something daring: They fell in love. Quakers and Baptists were expected to marry within their own church family. Daniel and Lucy married anyway, and lived in a home nestled between the farms of their parents. In order to marry Daniel, Lucy Read gave up her Baptist ways. She no longer wore bright clothing, sang, danced, or attended parties. Quakers, also known as Friends, were people who tried to live a quiet and simple life.

The Anthonys had eight children. Of the six who lived, four were daughters and two were sons. Susan Brownell Anthony was born on February 15, 1820. She was the second daughter born to the Anthonys. In those days, girls and women were considered necessary, but not as smart as boys or men. However, Susan was luckier than most girls. Her family was Quaker. Quakers treated men and women as equals. Girls as well as boys were encouraged to think for themselves. At the Friends Meeting House, women were allowed to speak at the church services, called meetings. Women could vote on church-related matters. At home, sons were not superior to daughters, and wives had almost as

Susan was born in this house built by her father,
Daniel Anthony, in Adams, Massachusetts.

much influence as husbands in making decisions. Outside the Quaker religion, women had none of these opportunities.

Daniel supported his growing family by starting a cotton mill. He employed young women, who boarded with the Anthonys. Susan did not see much of the workers because they worked at the mill from 6 A.M. to 6 P.M. every day except Sunday. While Daniel tended his businesses, Lucy Anthony and her children spent long hours cooking, cleaning, sewing, washing, ironing, and caring for the garden and chickens. They took care of all the mill workers in addition to their own family.

When Lucy Anthony was expecting her fourth child, she sent Guelma and Susan to stay at Grandmother Anthony's neighboring farm. Susan loved going to Grandmother's house. She made wonderful doughnuts, maple candy, and baked goods.

Workers in textile mills like that owned by Daniel Anthony used looms and other equipment. Young Susan did not understand why none of the supervisors in the mill were women, even though they were more familiar with the work and the machines.

When Susan and Guelma arrived at Grandmother's house, they were fascinated by a special house guest, Rhoda Brownell. Miss Brownell was staying with the Anthonys while she taught at the school that Grandfather Anthony ran.

"Can you teach me to read?" three-year-old Susan asked.

"Of course I can!" Miss Brownell replied.

Before long, Susan was reading. Unfortunately, she also contracted the childhood disease whooping cough. When she was well and could finally return home, she was excited to show her mother how she could read.

Instead of being excited to see Susan, her mother cried out, "What happened to your eyes? They are crossed!"

Lucy Anthony blamed Susan's crossed eyes on the whooping cough and the eye strain from reading. For the rest of her life, Susan was embarrassed about her eyes, even though her left eye eventually corrected itself and the turn of her right eye was hardly noticeable.

In 1826, Susan's father moved his family to Battenville, New York, to open and run a larger textile mill. When the Anthony family arrived there, Susan and her sisters were sent to the district school. In this school, the girls were seated at the back of the class and the boys were seated in the front. Everyone was taught to read, but only the boys were taught long division. One day after school, Susan asked her teacher to let her learn division.

"Why, Susan, don't worry your pretty head. Only the boys need to know division," he replied.

When Susan told her father she wasn't allowed to learn long division, he decided to start a school of his own where both boys and girls would be taught all the subjects. He hired good teachers and invited children of the community to attend for a small fee. Susan's favorite teacher, Mary Perkins, brought new books with pictures in them. Susan had never seen books with pictures.

"These books are wonderful!" Susan exclaimed as she flipped through the pages.

Miss Perkins did something else totally new with her students. She taught the boys and girls to exercise when they were tired of schoolwork.

Schooling for girls was unusual. Most parents didn't think girls needed much education. In fact, in the 1840s there was only one regular college (Oberlin, in Ohio) and one women's seminary (Mount Holyoke, in Massachusetts) where female students could receive a higher education.

Daniel Anthony believed that girls as well as boys should have a good education. In addition to his own children, Daniel also taught classes for those who worked for him. Susan gained a deep respect for education from him.

Susan was fascinated by her father's mills. She often visited to watch the workers. Her favorite worker was Sally Ann Hyatt. Sally Ann was the smartest person at the mill. She had a special talent for fixing machines when they broke down. Everyone, even the supervisor, who was a man, came to her for help.

After one of her visits to the mill, eleven-year-old Susan came to her father, her forehead wrinkled and her eyes serious.

"Father," Susan asked, "why do you have a man as supervisor when Sally Ann knows more than he does?"

"Supervision of labor has always been by men, Susan."

"But why?"

"Sally Ann deserves the job and the money. But it would not work. If Sally Ann were the supervisor, the men would probably quit and so would most of the women. They would refuse to work for her."

"It's not fair!" Susan pouted.

"It's wrong, but that is how it is right now," her father replied gently.

One evening while Susan was setting the table for dinner, she heard her father telling her mother, "Sally Ann Hyatt, one of my

Susan experienced inequality between boys and girls at a young age, when her schoolteacher, a man, told her that as a girl she did not need to learn long division. Here, a male schoolteacher instructs his class. If this class is anything like Susan's class was, then the boys and girls are not receiving an equal education.

spoolers, is ill. I'm going to need someone to take her place for two weeks."

Susan, now twelve years old, couldn't resist. "Please, Father, I know how to do the work! Can I take her place for two weeks?"

"No, no!" her sister Hannah joined in. "Let me do it!"

After drawing straws, Susan was allowed to work at the mill, but she had to split her wages with Hannah. At the end of two weeks she had earned $3. She gave Hannah her $1.50, and with her own money Susan bought her mother six blue china cups and saucers.

Susan's first real job was not at the factory but in the schoolroom. At fifteen, Susan became a teacher of children who attended school during the summer months. Next she taught in Easton in the home of a Quaker family for $1.00 a week plus board. Then she taught in a district school for $1.50 a week plus board.

When she was seventeen she went to a boarding school in Philadelphia, but in the spring of 1838, after only six months at school, her father's businesses failed and she went home. Susan and Guelma returned to teaching. They gave the money they earned to their father to save the mill. But the mill closed.

A year later, everything the Anthonys owned—their home and its contents, their clothes, even some eyeglasses—was put up for auction. Everything that had belonged to Lucy Anthony was considered the property of her husband and was used to pay his debts. Susan would never forget this injustice to her mother. She used $11 she had saved to buy back some of her parents' favorite things. Her mother's brother, Joshua Read, helped by buying and returning to Lucy some of the furniture and silver she had received as wedding gifts.

After the sale, Susan's family moved to Hardscrabble. Susan worked around the house baking, washing, spinning, and weaving. Although the family had little money, the years in Hardscrabble were happy. Their friends continued to call, and they were invited to many social affairs. During this time, Susan moved from place to place working as a teacher and governess. In 1845, when Susan was twenty-five years old, the Anthony family moved to Rochester, New York.

Lessons Learned. The lives of many people and the lessons they taught helped to form Susan's beliefs and values in her early years.

Susan's grandmothers were strong women. Grandmother Read spent her life running her farm and raising seven children. Her husband served ten years as a soldier, dabbled in politics, joined the Universalist faith, and spent his time at the local tavern giving his opinions. He was little help to his wife. It was Grandmother Read's intelligence and business sense that made the farm prosper.

On Susan's father's side, Grandmother and Great Grandmother Anthony had attained the High Seat in Quaker councils, a very important position in the Society of Friends.

From her mother, Lucy Read Anthony, Susan learned the hardships of frequent pregnancies, then raising six children and taking care of boarders. Lucy Anthony was a worn and silent person. Susan saw the injustice her mother suffered when all the money she earned by taking in boarders, and all her possessions, were legally her husband's. Susan believed that married women should have the right to keep what they earned and what they inherited.

Susan's father provided her with the best education possible and gave her a love of learning. Her father was also active in human-rights struggles. Susan learned to oppose alcohol and slavery by following his example and was introduced to the women's rights movement by both her parents.

At the age of twenty-six, Susan was appointed headmistress of the female department at Canajoharie Academy in upstate New York. She taught there from 1846 to 1849. During this time, she lived with her cousin Margaret Caldwell, a non-Quaker. Margaret taught Susan the fun of wearing colorful clothing and of attending the theater.

Margaret became ill after the birth of her fourth child, and Susan took care of her. Margaret's husband was self-centered and did little to support his wife during her illness. One day he complained of a headache. When Margaret told him she had a headache, too, he replied, "Oh, mine is the real headache, genuine pain, yours is a sort of natural consequence." A few weeks later Margaret died. Susan never forgot the way Margaret's husband had disregarded his wife's needs. Like many men in those days, he believed that only his needs were important.

From her teaching, Susan also learned lessons that influenced her life. Susan tolerated the humiliation of receiving lower wages than men who did the same work. While her salary was $2.50 a week plus board, men doing the same job earned three times as much. At a teachers' convention, the women always sat in the back, the men in front. During a convention in 1853, the men were asking each other why teachers were not respected like lawyers, ministers, and doctors. Susan B. Anthony asked to speak. Never had a woman asked to speak. Although both the men and women were surprised, the men decided she could speak. She

By the time Susan was working as headmistress at the Canajoharie Academy, she had broken away from the plain dress and way of living of her Quaker upbringing. She attended socials wearing this plaid dress, which was a colorful blue, purple, and brown.

said, "Do you not see that so long as society says woman has not brains enough to be a doctor, lawyer, or minister, but has ample ability to be a teacher, every man of you who chooses to teach tacitly admits ... that he has no more brains than a woman?"

For the next nine years she attended every state teachers' convention and campaigned for equal rights for women. She wanted women to be allowed to serve on committees, speak in public, hold office, and receive equal pay. She also believed that boys and girls should attend classes together. "If they [boys and girls] are allowed to attend picnics together, and balls, and dancing schools, and the opera, it certainly will not injure them to use chalk at the same blackboard."

Susan, the Reformer. Susan B. Anthony spent most of her life fighting for human rights. She was involved in three major reform movements: temperance, antislavery, and women's rights. Her interest in all three causes came from her understanding of what it was like to be treated unfairly.

In July 1848, at Seneca Falls, New York, two pioneers in women's rights, Elizabeth Cady Stanton and Lucretia Mott, organized a convention "to discuss the social, civil, and religious rights of women." It was the start of the American women's rights movement. Three hundred women attended and drafted the Declaration of Women's Rights and Sentiments, which called for the right of women to:

- own property
- speak freely
- sue for divorce
- enter educational and professional fields on an equal footing with men
- vote

Susan B. Anthony did not attend the convention of 1848 because she was teaching school. When the convention moved to Rochester two weeks later, Susan's parents attended and signed the Declaration of Sentiments, written by Elizabeth Cady Stanton. When they told Susan about the convention, she was eager to meet her.

Susan traveled to Seneca Falls for an abolitionist (antislavery) meeting. On the way home from a lecture, she was introduced to Elizabeth Cady Stanton. Mrs. Stanton invited Susan to visit her. Susan's visit changed the course of her life. Mrs. Stanton convinced Susan to attend a women's rights convention in 1852. At last Susan had the opportunity to hear competent women speaking on topics important to all women.

Susan joined Mrs. Stanton in the fight for women's equality. They would work as a team for more than fifty years. Susan supplied the facts, and Elizabeth wrote the speeches. They both spoke in person, but Susan was unmarried and therefore freer to travel, while Mrs. Stanton had seven children who needed her at home.

Another cause that Susan worked for was the temperance movement. The purpose of the temperance movement was to stop people from drinking alcohol. Many men drank heavily and then were cruel to their wives and children. Money needed to pay bills was often wasted on alcohol. Susan believed that alcohol was an evil that particularly impacted women. In 1849, Susan joined the Daughters of Temperance, an auxiliary group of the Sons of Temperance.

Susan made her first public speech at a women's temperance meeting in Canajoharie in 1849, attended by 200 men and women. Her speech was well received and elevated her to a place of leadership in the temperance movement.

This cartoon, used by a temperance group, shows why temperance was a special concern for women. Rather than working to support his family, the man has been drinking. Although it looks exaggerated, it was true that women had no place to turn if their husbands were neglectful or abusive, and alcohol made the problem worse.

In 1852 the Daughters of Temperance elected Susan as their delegate to a major temperance convention in Albany, New York. To her shock, the Sons of Temperance told the women delegates that they were invited to listen and learn, but not to speak. Furious, Susan left the meeting. Determined that women should have a major role in temperance, she and a group of women planned a statewide women's temperance convention to be held in April

1852. Susan's actions were cheered by Elizabeth Cady Stanton, a leader in a movement supporting women's rights. Elizabeth agreed to help Susan. More than 500 women attended the convention. The group established the Women's State Temperance Society. Men were welcome to join, but only women could hold office. Elizabeth Cady Stanton was elected president, and Susan was elected secretary. More than 1,000 women and men had joined the society by year's end.

Conflicts continued between the Sons of Temperance, now called the Men's State Temperance Society, and the women's society. Finally, the men who joined the Women's State Temperance Society outnumbered the women. With the help of sympathetic women, they voted a new name, The People's League, replaced Elizabeth as president, and reelected Susan as secretary. Susan and Elizabeth resigned from the organization.

Through her work in the temperance movement Susan became convinced that women needed to have equal rights, including the right to vote.

Following their work for temperance, Susan and Elizabeth Cady Stanton began a campaign to win property rights for married women in New York State. Both believed that women could accomplish little until they had the power to change laws. They organized a group of women to gather signatures on petitions from all over the state. After ten weeks they had almost 6,000 signatures.

Although their early efforts were not successful, they refused to give up. Finally in 1860 the legislature passed the Married Woman's Property Act, which gave women the right to own property, conduct their own businesses, control their own earnings, and share joint guardianship of children.

Susan did not attend the first women's rights convention in Seneca Falls, New York, in 1848. But her parents attended the convention in Rochester, which paved the way for Susan to meet its leader, Elizabeth Cady Stanton. This drawing shows Stanton addressing the first convention.

In the 1850s, the antislavery movement was growing, led by a group of reformers called abolitionists. Susan and her family were against slavery. They welcomed antislavery leaders such as William Lloyd Garrison, Wendell Phillips, and Frederick Douglass into their homes. A former slave, Frederick Douglass was a friend of Susan's father and became a close friend of Susan's. He visited the Anthony home often, and Susan, by listening to him talk, became convinced to join the fight to free all slaves.

Not everyone wanted the slaves to be freed. Some northern businessmen needed the cotton that southern slaves provided.

The Republican party wanted to exclude slavery from the western territories, leaving the South as it was. Some northerners feared that a division between the North and South might result if the abolitionists continued to call for freedom for all slaves. The abolitionists insisted that states with slaves should be excluded from the United States.

The abolitionists supported Susan's work for women. Because she was known for her work in the women's movement, Susan was hired by the abolitionists to organize the antislavery campaign in New York State. She recruited speakers, arranged meetings, and personally traveled from town to town to deliver the abolitionist message, "No Union With Slaveholders. Immediate and Unconditional Emancipation." The speakers were greeted by angry, defiant mobs who disrupted their speeches. Finally in Albany, New York, Mayor George Hornell Thacher took charge of their meetings. Seating himself on the platform with his revolver across his knees, he told Susan to open the meeting. For the first time, the speakers delivered their messages without interruption.

The Civil War caused the women's movement to be put on hold. In 1863 the women formed the Women's National Loyal League, which started a petition demanding freedom for slaves. The women collected 400,000 signatures and raised $3,000 for the Union. At the end of the war, the Thirteenth Amendment was passed, freeing the slaves.

Susan wanted the abolitionists and women's rights workers to campaign together for voting rights for both women and blacks. The proposed Fourteenth Amendment, which stated that the former slaves were citizens, and had a section about voting, referred to voters as "male citizens." Susan and Elizabeth Cady Stanton felt that the wording was a huge step backward. At the Women's Rights Convention of 1866, the Women's Rights Association was renamed the American Equal Rights Society. The goal was to work toward securing the vote for women and blacks.

However, most abolitionists felt that it was the black man's hour, and suggested that the women work only to get voting rights for black men. Abolitionist Wendell Phillips led the argument, saying that the fight for woman suffrage would weaken the cause of black suffrage. He said that the word "male" would have to stay in the Fourteenth Amendment at least for the time being. But Susan would not hear of it. "I would sooner cut off my right hand than ask for the ballot for the black man and not for woman," she stated.

Susan campaigned to have the words "male citizens" removed from the Fourteenth Amendment. Her efforts failed. The Fourteenth Amendment was ratified in 1868 in its original form.

When the Fifteenth Amendment was introduced it stated: "The right of citizens of the United States to vote shall not be denied or abridged…on account of race, color, or previous condition of servitude." But the word "sex" was omitted. Susan and her followers tried to get the wording changed, but again they failed. The amendment was ratified in February 1870.

In May 1869 the women's movement split when Susan and Elizabeth Cady Stanton organized the National Woman Suffrage Association, which was open to women members only. Its goal was passage of a constitutional amendment granting women the right to vote.

Susan B. Anthony and Elizabeth Cady Stanton worked together closely for more than fifty years on behalf of women's rights.

In November 1869, Lucy Stone and her husband Henry Blackwell, Amelia Bloomer, and a more conservative group of women formed the American Woman Suffrage Association. Although they wanted the vote for women, they believed, unlike Anthony and Stanton, that the passage of the Fourteenth and Fifteenth Amendments was a step in the right direction.

Failure Is Impossible. Susan B. Anthony spent most of her life working for women's rights. She became the publisher of a woman-suffrage newspaper, *The Revolution*. In 1881, Susan and

Elizabeth Cady Stanton published the first of six books, *History of Woman Suffrage*. In 1872, Susan and her group organized their daring attempt to vote, which they succeeded at, even though they were arrested and Susan was tried and found guilty.

In 1888, Susan founded the International Council of Women. The first international meeting was held in Washington, D.C. The event, organized and planned by the National Woman Suffrage Association, provided an opportunity for women from Europe, Asia, and the United States to discuss the movement for equality, and to give women a sense of the power of working together. Susan, Elizabeth Cady Stanton, and Lucy Stone were together on the platform. Young members from both the National and American Woman Suffrage Associations urged their organizations to unite. In 1890 the two groups reconciled and formed the National American Woman Suffrage Association (NAWSA). In 1892, Susan was elected president.

Through much of her life, people made fun of Susan when she tried to speak in public. She faced angry crowds when she worked to free the slaves. Eggs were thrown at her, and a dummy representing her was dragged through the streets. She was shamed and belittled for being a woman who chose to speak out about what she saw as unfair.

But Susan refused to quit. She traveled through snowstorms, she stayed in cold buildings, and she spoke wherever she could find a place for women (and men) to gather.

Finally, during the 1890s, four states—Wyoming, Colorado, Idaho, and Utah—gave women the right to vote. Susan and her reformers were making an impact.

Just as Susan was often jeered at her public speaking engagements, the woman-suffrage movement prompted ridicule from many directions. This cartoon was published in 1869. What does the cartoonist seem to be saying about those involved in the movement?

On her eightieth birthday, in 1900, Susan B. Anthony resigned as president of NAWSA. However, she continued speaking in support of women's right to vote. In an interview in 1901 she said: "We women must be up and doing: I can hardly sit still when I think of the great work waiting to be done."

In 1902, realizing that her age was making it harder for her to continue her work, she said: "...There is so much yet to be done, I see so many things I would like to do and say, but I must leave it for the younger generation. We old fighters have pre-pared the way. ..."

Although her health was failing, Susan was determined to attend the NAWSA convention in Baltimore in February 1906. She listened to testimonials praising her years of work. M. Carey Thomas, who was the president of Bryn Mawr College and longtime friend of Susan's, said:

> Other women reformers ... have given part of their time and energy. [Susan B. Anthony] has given to the cause of women every year, every month, every day, every hour, every moment of her whole life, and every dollar she could beg or earn....
> ...To you, Miss Anthony, belongs by right, as to no other woman in the world's history, the love and gratitude of all women in every country of the civilized globe. We, your daughters in the spirit, rise up today and call you blessed...."

Following the testimonials, Susan gave her last public speech.

From Baltimore she traveled to Washington, D.C., for a celebration of her eighty-sixth birthday. Here she gave her friends her final message:

> There have been others also just as true and devoted to the cause—I wish I could name every one—but with such women consecrating their lives, failure is impossible.

Four years before her death in 1906, Susan B. Anthony stated,
"There is so much yet to be done, I see so many things I would like
to do and say, but I must leave it for the younger generation.
We old fighters have prepared the way."

The younger generation did, indeed, take up the fight, staging numerous marches and demonstrations. This parade took place in New York City in 1911. Finally, in 1920, the Nineteenth Amendment was passed, granting women the right to vote.

Susan B. Anthony died on March 13, 1906.

August 26, 1920, fourteen years after Susan B. Anthony's death, was a day that changed the lives of women forever. The Nineteenth Amendment to the U.S. Constitution became law, and women were granted the right to vote.

The Nineteenth Amendment, named for Susan B. Anthony, came after 72 years of hard work. During those years, women presented 56 referenda to male voters; campaigned with 19 successive U.S. Congresses; led 47 attempts to get state constitutional conventions to write woman suffrage into their state constitutions; tried 277 times to get political parties to put woman suffrage on their planks at state conventions, and 30 times to get suffrage on their party planks at presidential conventions.

Most of us today will never know the sacrifices and struggles of the women who worked to convince male politicians, clergy, husbands, and fathers of the discrimination against women.

> Can you blame the pioneers...Elizabeth Cady Stanton, Lucy Stone, and all those others, when we saw with clear eyes the future spread out before us?...We were not seers, but we did see that something must be done for women, and...I had to do my part. That is all.
> Susan B. Anthony, 1905

THOSE WHO MADE
A DIFFERENCE

Antoinette Brown Blackwell (1825–1921), a graduate of Oberlin College, became the first woman ordained as a minister. Active all her adult life in equal rights and justice for all, Antoinette lived long enough to cast her first and only ballot at the age of ninety-five.

Carrie Chapman Catt (1859–1947) took part in the campaign for women's rights in South Dakota, attended the National American Woman Suffrage Association convention in 1890, and led the campaign supporting a referendum giving women the right to vote in Colorado in 1893. As president of the Organization Committee of NAWSA, she saw that every state and territory was brought into NAWSA, helped Idaho become a suffrage state in 1896, and succeeded Susan B. Anthony as president of NAWSA in 1900. Carrie played a major role in the passage of the Nineteenth Amendment and was responsible for NAWSA's transformation into the League of Women Voters.

Sarah (1792–1873) and **Angelina** (1805–1879) **Grimké** grew up on a South Carolina plantation. They tried to improve the lives of slaves and women. When this didn't work in the South, they moved to the North. Their goal was to convince people that women should take part in government. On February 21, 1838, Angelina became the first woman to address a legislative body, urging the lawmakers to end the system of slavery. Sarah and Angelina traveled throughout New England telling all who would listen that slavery was evil, and that free people had a moral duty to end it. Sarah wrote *Letters on the Equality of the Sexes and the Condition of Women,* published in 1838. It was the first serious study by an American woman on women's rights.

Lucretia Mott (1793–1880) was a pioneer in women's rights. A Quaker minister and a gifted speaker, she was active in the antislavery cause and played an important role in the Underground Railroad. In 1848, along with Elizabeth Cady Stanton, Martha C. Wright, Jane Hunt, and Mary Ann McClintock, Mott planned the first women's rights conference to be held in the United States. It occurred at Seneca Falls, New York, in 1848. Mott was a champion against injustice and advocated equal rights for all persons—women, blacks, Indians—until her death in 1880 at the age of eighty-seven.

Alice Paul (1885–1977), a Quaker, joined the suffrage movement and organized the National Woman's Party in 1916. The National Woman's Party used radical tactics to campaign for the vote, such as marches, chaining themselves to fences, picketing, and hunger strikes. After the passage of the Nineteenth Amendment, she began a campaign for an Equal Rights Amendment to guarantee total equality for women.

Elizabeth Cady Stanton (1815–1902) first discovered unfairness to women when she studied her father's law books and watched as her father, a judge, was unable to help women because the laws favored men. In 1848, Elizabeth helped plan the Seneca Falls Conference and was the author of the Declaration of Sentiments, which included a request to change the laws to allow women to vote. In 1851 she met Susan B. Anthony and worked with her for fifty years to get equal rights for women. Elizabeth Cady Stanton died in 1902, eighteen years before women achieved the right to vote.

Lucy Stone (1818–1893) began teaching at the age of sixteen. She was angry to be paid less than men for equal work. In 1843 she went to college at Oberlin, Ohio, the only college where men and women, both black and white, were allowed to attend together. She graduated in 1847 and began a career as an abolitionist. She became a lecturer for the abolitionists but found she couldn't keep the subjects of slavery and women's rights apart. The abolitionists who hired her were annoyed, so she agreed to speak against slavery on weekends and on women's rights the rest of the week. Lucy served as president of the Women's National Loyal League, helped found the American Equal Rights Association, established the American Woman Suffrage Association, and started a magazine, *The Woman's Journal*. In 1890 the American and National Woman Suffrage Associations united. After Lucy's death in 1893, her husband Henry and her daughter Alice continued the work she had begun.

Sojourner Truth (1797?–1883), a former slave who gained her freedom in 1827, fought against slavery and for women's rights. At a women's conference in 1851, a clergyman ridiculed the weakness of women. Furious, Sojourner rose to say:

> That man over there says women need to be helped into carriages and lifted over ditches, and to have the best place everywhere. Well, nobody ever helped me into carriages or over ditches, or gives me the best place. And ain't I a woman? I have ploughed and planted and gathered into barns and no man could head me. And ain't I a woman? I can work as much and eat as much as a man—when I could get it—and bear the lash as well. And ain't I a woman? I have borne thirteen children and seen most of 'em sold into slavery and when I cried out my mother's grief, none but Jesus heard me. And ain't I a woman?

Sojourner believed that the rights of blacks and women were bound together.

AUTHOR'S NOTE

A statue of three great leaders of the women's movement—Susan B. Anthony, Elizabeth Cady Stanton, and Lucretia Mott—was commissioned in 1921. The day after the statue was dedicated, it was moved from the rotunda in the Capitol building in Washington, D.C., to an area called the Crypt located on a lower level. In 1995, organizers for the seventy-fifth anniversary of the passage of the Nineteenth Amendment appealed to Congress to have it moved into a prominent place in the rotunda along with other liberators of democracy such as George Washington, Abraham Lincoln, Roger Williams of Rhode Island, and Martin Luther King, Jr.

On the day of the celebration in August 1995, women gathered around the statue to honor the three women who did so much for the liberation of all women. Where did they gather? In the Crypt at the Capitol, a few feet from the rest rooms and gift shop.

Finally, in May 1997, the statue of the three women suffragists was moved to the rotunda for a one-year visit. It was moved because there are no statues of women in the rotunda. A carving

Susan B. Anthony was commemorated with a dollar coin in 1979,
the only woman to be so honored. She and other women's rights leaders
have also been featured on postage stamps.

of Pocahontas and paintings of Pocahontas and Martha Washington are the only tributes to women there. About $80,000 was raised by the Woman Suffrage Statue Campaign to move the statue.

Arlys Endres, a fourth-grader in Phoenix, Arizona, conducted her own fundraising campaign to help move the statue. She spent five hours a week writing to neighbors, relatives, and celebrities asking donors to send in their Susan B. Anthony dollar coins or

The statue jokingly called "Three Women in a Bathtub" was sculpted in 1921 by Adelaide Johnson. It shows Elizabeth Cady Stanton, Susan B. Anthony, and Lucretia Mott.

Federal Reserve notes with the initials SBA written on them. She collected nearly $2,000 toward the fund.

Critics of the statue claim that the carving is coarse, rough, and unfinished. A slab of uncarved stone juts up behind the three faces. It's jokingly called "Three Women in a Tub." But perhaps the sculptor intentionally left an unfinished slab of rock to represent the unfinished work toward equal rights for women.

When told the statue has been called ugly, Arlys Endres responded, "The statue is from an ugly time—women didn't have the right to vote."

PLACES TO VISIT

Susan B. Anthony House, 17 Madison Street, Rochester, New York. Susan lived in this house from 1866 until her death in 1906. Photographs and memorabilia portray the events of Susan's life and her work in the woman-suffrage movement.

The National Women's Hall of Fame, 76 Fall Street, Seneca Falls, New York.

Women's Rights National Historical Park, 136 Fall Street, Seneca Falls, New York. This park contains a visitors' center, the remains of the Wesleyan Chapel, and the Elizabeth Cady Stanton house.

IMPORTANT DATES

1820	Susan Brownell Anthony born near Adams, Massachusetts (February 15)
1826	Anthony family moves to Battenville, New York
1832	Susan works for two weeks in her father's mill
1835	Susan begins teaching
1837	Susan goes to boarding school in Philadelphia
1838	Father's business fails; Susan returns home
1845	Anthony family moves to Rochester, New York
1846–1849	Susan is headmistress of "female department" at Canajoharie Academy
1848	First Women's Rights Convention held at Seneca Falls, New York (July 19–20)
1849	Susan joins Daughters of Temperance in Canajoharie and gives first public speech
1851	Susan meets Elizabeth Cady Stanton
1852	Susan founds Women's State Temperance Society (New York)
1853	Men take over Women's State Temperance Society; Susan and Elizabeth Cady Stanton quit organization; Susan speaks on education at New York State Teachers Association Convention

1853–1860	Susan and Elizabeth Cady Stanton travel across New York State lecturing on women's property rights
1860	New York State passes the Married Woman's Property Act (March 20)
1856–1864	Susan works for the abolition of slavery
1866	Susan works to get the words "male citizens" removed from the Fourteenth Amendment
1868–1870	Susan publishes *The Revolution,* a woman-suffrage newspaper
1869	Women form two competing groups, the National Woman Suffrage Association and the American Woman Suffrage Association
1872	U.S. marshal arrests Susan for illegal voting
1881	Mrs. Stanton and Susan publish the first volume of *History of Woman Suffrage*
1888	Susan founds the International Council of Women
1890	Wyoming admitted as first woman-suffrage state; National and American Woman Suffrage Associations merge and become National American Woman Suffrage Association (NAWSA)
1892	Susan becomes president of NAWSA
1906	Susan attends her final NAWSA convention in Baltimore; Susan attends her eighty-sixth birthday celebration in Washington, D.C., where she says "failure is impossible"; Susan Brownell Anthony dies (March 13)
1920	The Nineteenth Amendment, giving women the right to vote, is ratified

FURTHER READING

Clinton, Susan. *The Story of Susan B. Anthony.* Chicago: Childrens Press, 1986.

Connell, Kate. *They Shall Be Heard: Susan B. Anthony and Elizabeth Cady Stanton.* Austin, TX: Raintree Steck-Vaughn Publishers, 1993.

Cooper, Ilene. *Susan B. Anthony.* New York: Franklin Watts, 1984.

Faber, Doris. *Lucretia Mott.* Champaign, IL: Garrard Publishing Company, 1971.

Gleiter, Jan, and Kathleen Thompson. *Elizabeth Cady Stanton.* Milwaukee: Raintree Children's Books, 1988.

Levin, Pamela. *Susan B. Anthony: Fighter for Women's Rights.* New York: Chelsea House Publishers, 1993.

McPherson, Stephanie Sammartino. *I Speak for the Women: A Story About Lucy Stone.* Minneapolis: Carolrhoda Books, Inc., 1992.

Weisberg, Barbara. *Susan B. Anthony.* New York: Chelsea House Publishers, 1988.

INDEX